My Cat

Nancy Hicer

Rosen REAL READERS

Rosen Classroom™
New York

1

This is my friend's cat.

His name is Sam.

I am watching Sam

while my friend is away.

I wake up early to feed Sam.

Sam eats cat food.

He eats cat food from a bowl.

I give Sam water.

Sam needs to drink water.

Sam takes a nap.

Sam sleeps in a basket.

Sam wakes up.

He plays with a toy.

Sam lies near the window.

He looks outside.

Sam goes outside to play.

Sam sees a tree.

Sam climbs the tree.

Sam comes home.
I feed Sam cat food
for dinner.

After a long day,
Sam is tired.
Sam goes to sleep
for the night.

Words to Know

basket

bowl

cat

food

toy